AIR MINISTRY.

DIRECTORATE OF RESEARCH.

H. 706.

Enemy Engine Report No. 16.

CENTRAL HOUSE,
KINGSWAY,
W.C. 2.

Reduction Gears
USED ON
Five-Engined Giant Gotha Bomber.

JUNE, 1919.

The Naval & Military Press Ltd

Published by
The Naval & Military Press Ltd
5 Riverside, Brambleside, Bellbrook
Industrial Estate, Uckfield, East Sussex,
TN22 1QQ England

Tel: +44 (0) 1825 749494
Fax: +44 (0) 1825 765701

www.naval-military-press.com
www.military-genealogy.com

*In reprinting in facsimile from the original, any imperfections are inevitably reproduced
and the quality may fall short of modern type and cartographic standards.*

AIR MINISTRY.

DIRECTORATE OF RESEARCH.

H. 706.

Enemy Engine Report No. 16.

CENTRAL HOUSE,
KINGSWAY,
W.C. 2.

Reduction Gears
USED ON
Five-Engined Giant Gotha Bomber.

JUNE, 1919.

CORRIGENDUM SLIP.
H. 706.

"Reduction Gears used on 5-engined Giant Gotha Bomber".

on page 8. Fig.11 Sketch of Thermo Couple read:-
                Fig:11 Sketch of Resistance Thermometer

Paragraph headed "Thermo Couple" should read as follows:-

Resistance Thermometer

    Beneath the oil sump of the gear case proper an electrical resistance thermometer is fitted, which communicates with a dial on the dashboard. There is no apparent means of controlling the draught of air through the oil radiator. The construction of this electrical thermometer is shown in Fig.11.

Reduction Gears

used on

Five-Engined Giant Gotha Bomber.

REDUCTION GEARS

USED ON

Five-Engined Gotha Bomber.

LIST OF ILLUSTRATIONS.

Fig.
1. Long Type Reduction Gear.
2. Underneath View of Reduction Gear.
3. Long Type (Pusher) Propeller Shaft.
4. Short Type (Tractor) Propeller Shaft and Pinion.
5. Driving Pinion and Bearings.
6. Sketch of Front End Roller Bearing and Propeller Hub Flange.
7. Propeller Shaft, Gears, and Flexible Coupling (dismantled).
8. Parts of Gear-Case (dismantled).
9. View of Oil Radiator and Oil Pump.
10. Oil Filter.
11. Sketch of Thermo-Couple.
12. Sectional General Arrangement of Reduction Gear and Lubrication System.

Fig. 1. Complete Reduction Gear (Long Type).

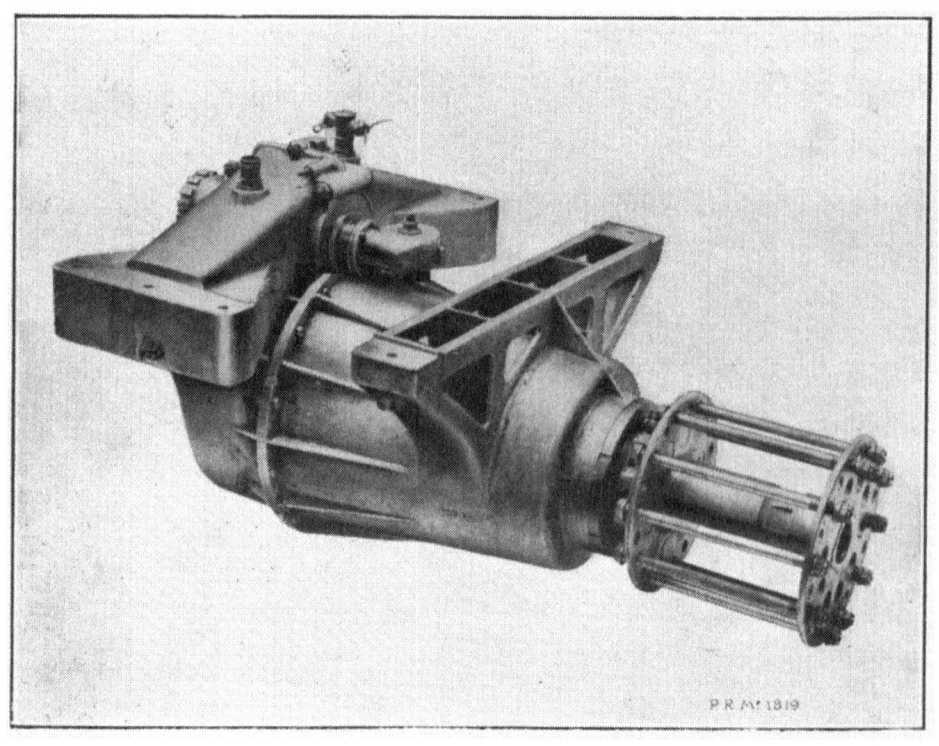

Fig. 2. Underneath View of Reduction Gear, showing oil pump drive and thermo-couple.

Report on Reduction Gears used on Five-Engined Giant Gotha Bomber.

INTRODUCTORY NOTE.

The following illustrated report on the design and construction of an interesting type of oil-cooled reduction gear, used in the most recent enemy Giant Bomber, is based on a detailed examination of the damaged parts taken from a five-engined Gotha Bomber which was brought down near Talmas on August 10, 1918. Unfortunately, the machine was too badly damaged for reconstruction owing to the explosion of one of its bombs.

Five of these massive reduction gears, which are constructed as separate units, were used in the machine—one for each of the five standard 300 H.P. Maybach engines, a report on which has already been issued.

The engines were arranged in the machine in the following manner:—One engine was installed in the nose of the fuselage, driving a tractor air screw, whilst on each side of the machine, and supported by the wings, was a pair of long engine bearers, built up of laminated wood, each pair carrying two engines in tandem, driving tractor and pusher air screws.

Two types of reduction gear were employed, which differ only in their overall dimensions and the length of the propeller shafts, the difference between which is indicated in Figs. 3 and 4. The longer type was used for the pusher screws in order to obviate the necessity of cutting away a portion of the trailing edge of the main planes, whilst the short type was used for the three tractor screws, and fitted close up to the front end of the engine.

All the reduction gears were very badly damaged, except one of the longer type, views of which are shown in Figs. 1 and 2.

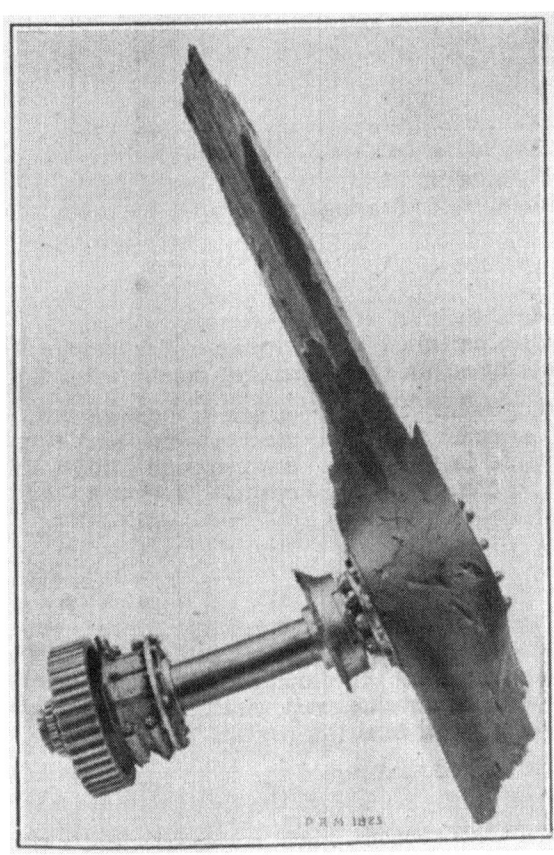

Fig. 3.
Long Type (Pusher) Propeller Shaft.
Pusher Screw and Driven Pinion.

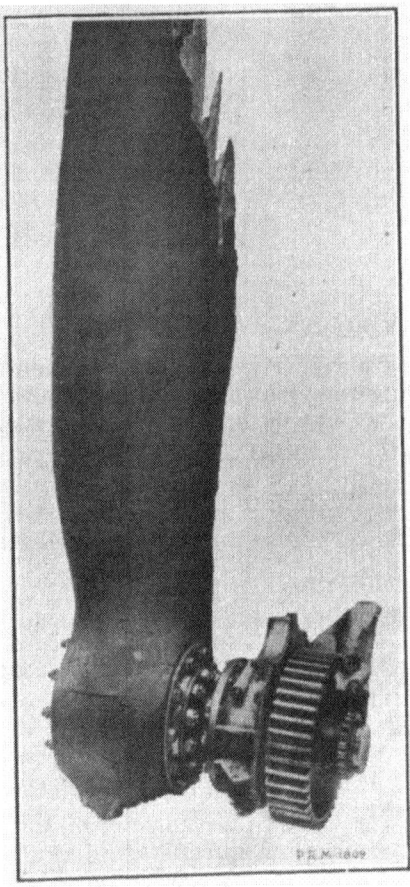

Fig. 4.
Short Type (Tractor) Propeller Shaft and Pinion.

GENERAL DESCRIPTION.

In each reduction gear the ratio of engine to propeller speed is the same, the gear reduction being approximately half engine speed—i.e., 41/21—and, as shown in the illustrations, the design of the reduction gear is such that the axis of the propeller is raised 217 mm. above that of the crankshaft.

The use of these reduction gears necessitates the fitting of a light flywheel to each of the engines. The flywheels are 400 mm. in diameter, and are made of cast-iron. On the inside of each flywheel is fitted the female portion of a flexible coupling. These couplings are of a similar design to the couplings used with the 240 H.P. Maybach engines in the earlier types of Zeppelin airships, and consist of a male and female drum made of aluminium, each furnished with circumferential recesses, into which are fitted a series of twelve flat leather pads or blocks which take the drive. These leather blocks are built up of a number of small strips of tough leather clamped and rivetted together by two steel plates at the edges. The general design of the flexible driving coupling is shown in section in the General Arrangement Drawing, Fig. 12. The male portion of the coupling, which is also of aluminium, is secured by eight bolts, and engaged by means of sixteen splines, with the flanged end of a sleeve, which is mounted on the rear end extension of the driving pinion. This sleeve is fitted to the driving spur pinion extension by six splines, and is secured in position by a screwed plug, as shown in section in the drawing.

Fig. 5. Driving Pinion and Bearings.

DRIVING SPUR PINION.

Plain spur gears are used, and are designed with a pitch of 22 mm. (7 module). The driving spur pinion has 21 teeth, and is shown dismantled with its two roller bearings in Fig. 5. The pitch circle diameter is 147 mm., the width of the teeth 75 mm.

As shown in section in the General Arrangement, the spur pinion is hollow, and is machined inside to a diameter of 92 mm. The spur pinion is mounted on single race bearings—one on each side—which are contained in gun-metal housings, and fitted with a helical oil groove and felt oil retainer at the rear end.

PROPELLER SHAFT AND SPUR WHEEL.

Referring to Fig. 12, it will be seen that the spur wheel is spigotted into the rear end of the tubular propeller shaft by a long splined extension of the spur wheel hub. Six shallow splines are cut on the extension, which is pressed into the propeller shaft, and secured by a screwed plug. The extension spigot of the spur wheel is pressed into the propeller shaft as far as a shoulder machined on the spur wheel hub.

The pitch-circle diameter of the spur wheel is 287 mm., and the tooth formation is, of course, also 7 module.

Taking the normal speed of the standard 300 H.P. Maybach engine at 1,400 r.p.m., the torque of the driving spur-pinion equals 1,125 lbs., which gives a loading on the teeth of 4,665 ft. lbs. per min.

The approximate normal H.P. of this engine at 1,400 R.P.M. has for this calculation been taken at 300 instead of 294.4—the actual figure given on test.

Fig. 6. Sketch of Front End Roller Bearing and Propeller Hub Flange, showing the two helical oil retainers.

BEARINGS.

The propeller shaft runs in three single race roller-bearings, one at each side of the spur wheel and one at the front end of the shaft. The bearings are carried in well-designed gun-metal housings fitted into the cast aluminium gear case. A large double-thrust ball-race is provided behind the centre radial load-bearing next to the spur wheel, the thrust washers being held in position on the propeller shaft and in the housing by screwed collars.

Fig. 7. Propeller Shaft, Gears, and Flexible Coupling.

The outside diameter of the propeller shaft is 92 mm., and the inside is machined to 82 mm. diameter in the centre between the front and middle bearings, where the shaft is parallel. The front end of the propeller shaft is bored taper to 96 mm. diameter, where it terminates in a flange 185 mm. diameter, to which the propeller hub is bolted by ten bolts let into the face of the hub rear flange.

A detail sketch of the front end roller bearing is given in Fig. 6, which illustrates the method of locking the roller bearing in position in its housing, and shows the two helical oil-retaining grooves. These helical grooves or worms are provided to circulate and retain grease, which is periodically injected through the small pipe by a grease gun, the front bearing being outside the main oil circulation of the gears.

Felt oil retaining washers are provided in the bearing locking rings, as shown in the sketch.

A photograph of the dismantled parts of the propeller shaft, gears, flexible coupling, etc., is shown in Fig. 7.

Fig. 8. Parts of Gear Case, dismantled.

GEAR CASE.

The gear case consists of three massive aluminium castings, as shown in the photograph, Fig. 8. The feet cast on the bottom of the case are bolted to the long engine bearers when installed in the machine. The rear or engine-end of the case is split vertically, and is in two parts, bolted together by the usual type of flanged joints, whilst the conical front portion of the case is a single casting, and is attached to the divided part of the case at the rear end by twelve 8 mm. bolts. These bolts, it is interesting to note, are made of a special aluminium alloy resembling duralumin. (A copy of the metallurgical analysis of the bolts, which are also used to fix the thrust-race housing to the case, is included in this report.)

The overall dimensions of the reduction gear are as follows:—
  Length   ...   .   1025 mm.
  Breadth   ...   .   675 mm.
  Height   ...   .   535 mm.

The weights of the gear case and its attachments are as follows:—
  Gear case (long type)   ...   ...   278.00 lbs.
  Oil radiator and pump   ...   ...   12.75 lbs.
                                                  ...   290.75 lbs.
  Flywheel   ...   .   37.00 lbs.

  Total weight of complete gear   ...   327.75 lbs.

or the equivalent of 1.09 lbs. per B.H.P. when used with a standard 300 H.P. Maybach engine.

LUBRICATION.

OIL RADIATOR AND PUMP.—A separate oil radiator is used in conjunction with each reduction gear. These are roughly of a semi-circular shape, and are slung underneath the main transverse members of the engine bearers, so that the radiator comes immediately beneath the large feet of the gear case. This radiator is constructed entirely of steel, and embraces 67 tubes of 24 mm. internal diameter, giving a total cooling area of 7,101.36 sq. cm. These are expanded and sweated into the end plates, to one of which is fitted a stout flange, against which is bolted a small gear pump. The pump circulates the oil from the gear case through the radiator, and is driven by a small worm-gear and flexible shaft from the front end of the spur pinion, the shaft and its casing being similar to those employed for engine revolution counters. Details of the oil pump and drive are shown in the sectional arrangement.

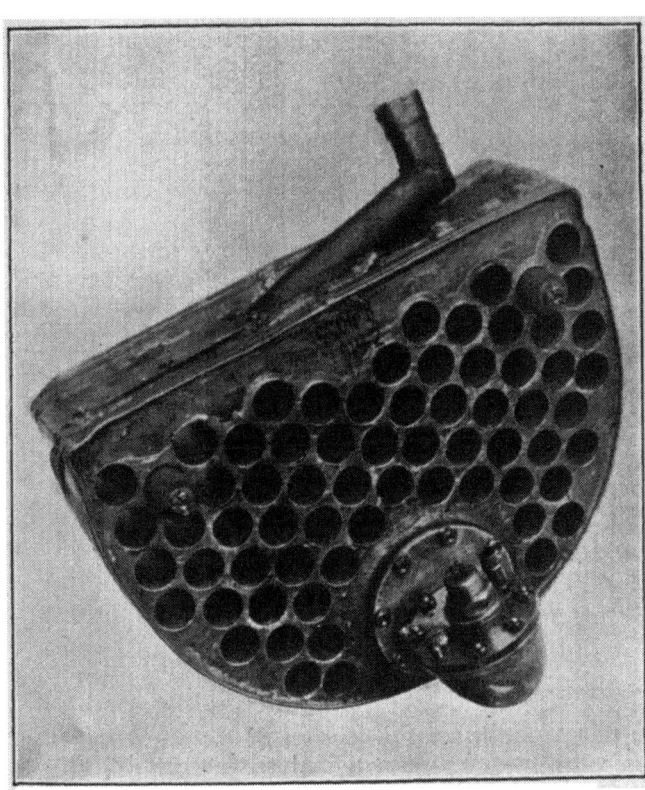

Fig. 9. View of Oil Radiator and Oil Pump.

Fig. 10. Oil Filter.

LUBRICATION SYSTEM.

In action, the efficient lubrication of the spur gears and their bearings is assured by the constant supply of cooled oil from the radiator below the gear case (a separate test report of which is attached). Oil is forced by the pump through an external pipe to the front of the main roller and thrust bearings, and also fed on to the spur gears through a union screwed into the top of the case, the oil returning by gravity through the case to the oil radiator below.

OIL FILTER.

Fitted on each gear case, and working in connection with the oil circulation is a filter of the type shown in Fig. 10.

TEST OF OIL PUMP.

A separate test has been carried out on the oil pump, and a curve taken of the delivery at constant speed against varying pressures. The pump was driven at 140 R.P.M., and the delivery taken at pressures varying between 10 and 60 lbs. per sq. in. with the following results:—

Pressure in lbs. sq. in.	10	20	30	40	50	60	R.P.M. 140.
Delivery in pints per hour	76	68	63.5	57	55.0	46.4	

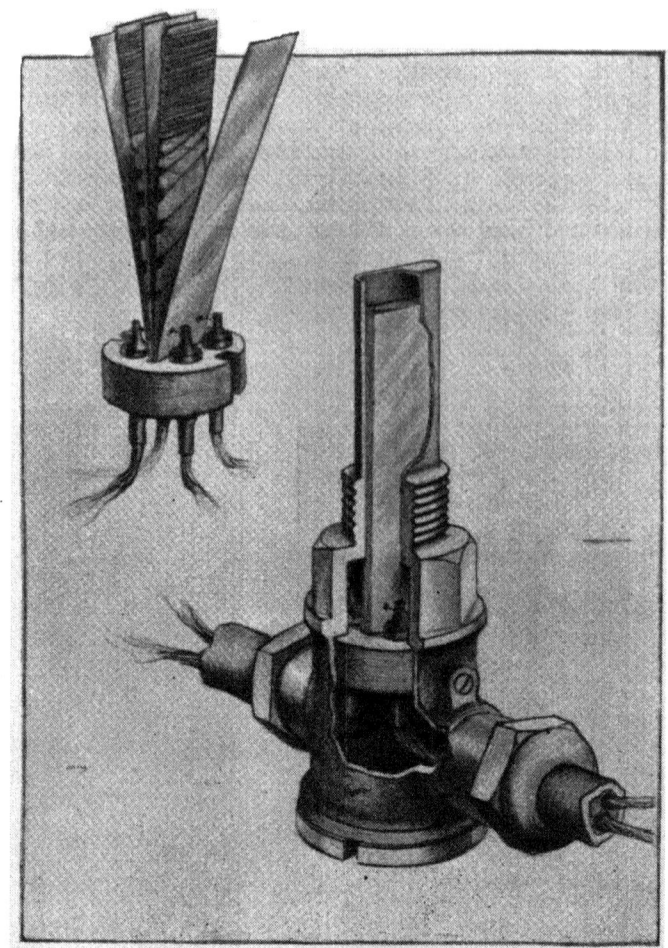

Fig. 11. Sketch of ~~Thermo-Couple~~ Resistance Thermometer.

THERMO-COUPLE.

Beneath the oil sump of the gear case proper an interesting design of electrical thermometer, or thermo-couple, is fitted, which communicates with a dial on the dashboard. It is a little difficult to see what object can be served by this thermo-couple, unless it be to indicate the desirability of throttling down a little in the event of the oil getting unduly hot; there is no apparent means of controlling the draught of air through the oil radiator. The construction of this electrical thermometer is shown in Fig. 11.

PROPELLER HUB.

The propeller hub is of the same construction as that used on the standard 300 H.P. Maybach engines, but is, of course, of very much larger proportions.

Leading particulars of the design and dimensions are given in the data at the end of the report.

As the air screws revolve at half engine speed, and have therefore a moderately light centrifugal load, they are made of a common wood which would scarcely be safe for direct driving screws.

Although fitted to 300 H.P. Maybach engines, they are marked 260 p.s. (h.p.) Mercedes. The diameter is 14.2 ft., and the pitch 10.82 ft. for the pusher screw, but unfortunately, owing to the propellers being badly damaged, not only by the crash, but by fire, it is not possible to state whether the tractor screws are of the same dimensions and pitch.

The construction is very interesting; each screw is made of seventeen laminations of what appears to be soft pine, and these laminations are themselves in pieces, and do not run continuously from tip to tip. They are, of course, staggered, so that the joints in successive layers do not coincide. Two plies of very thin birch veneer are wrapped round the blades. The grain of this veneer runs across the blade instead of along it.

METALLURGICAL ANALYSIS ON ALUMINIUM ALLOY BOLTS.
REPORT No. O.6/3420.

Results of a chemical analysis and tensile test on the reduction gear bolts are given below.

CHEMICAL ANALYSIS.

Copper	3.75 per cent.
Tin	0.91 per cent.
Zinc	Nil.
Magnesium	0.80 per cent.
Iron	0.23 per cent.
Aluminium (by diff.)	94.31 per cent.

TENSILE TEST.

Diameter	.111 in.
Yield stress	18.9 tons/sq. in.
Ultimate stress	26.3 tons/sq. in.
Elongation, per cent.	30.0.
Reduction of area, per cent.	12.0.

The material resembles Duralumin.

GENERAL ANALYSIS OF WEIGHTS.

Propeller hub, complete with shaft, flange bolts	38 lbs.
,, shaft and ring nuts	20.75 lbs.
Spur wheel, with shaft nuts	33.8 lbs.
Roller bearing retainer rings and housings (propeller end)	16.5 lbs.
Roller bearing and thrust race retainer ring and housing (central)	22.45 lbs.
Roller bearing and housing (spur wheel)	7.125 lbs.
Spur pinion and nut	20.8 lbs.
Roller bearing thrust race and housing (pump drive end)	5.0 lbs.
Screwed extension for pump drive, with thrust race retainer ring and worm	1.5 lbs.
Pump drive and casing	1.25 lbs.
Roller bearing retainer ring and housing (engine end)	4.375 lbs.
Male part of clutch, with driving dog	21.75 lbs.
Gear case, complete with bolts	77.7 lbs.
Total	271.00 lbs.
Oil pump and radiator	12.75 lbs.
Female portion of flexible coupling, with bolts	7 lbs.
Reduction gear, complete	290.75 lbs.
Flywheel	37 lbs.
Total weight of complete reduction gear, with flywheel	327.75 lbs.
Weight per B.H.P. (300 B.H.P. at 1,400 R.P.M.)	1.09 lbs.

GENERAL DATA.

DRIVING SHAFT.

Spur pinion, module	7.
,, ,, number of teeth	21.
,, ,, pitch-circle diameter	147 mm.
,, ,, width of teeth	75 mm.
,, ,, depth of teeth	15.1 mm.
Torque (at 1,400 R.P.M.)	1,125 lbs.
Loading on teeth (at 1,400 R.P.M.)	4,665 ft. lbs. per min.
Wheel bored (diameter)	92 mm.
Spur pinion extension, external diameter	65.0 mm.
,, ,, ,, internal diameter	40.0 mm.
,, ,, ,, number of splines	6.
,, ,, ,, depth of splines	4.0 mm.
Driving dog sleeve, diameter	78.0 mm.

Front and Rear Bearings.

Type	Roller.
Rollers, number	18.
,, diameter	14.0 mm.
,, width	14.0 mm.
Bronze housings, external diameter	126.0 mm.
,, ,, internal diameter	120.0 mm.

PROPELLER SHAFT.

SPUR WHEEL.

Spur wheel, module	7.
,, ,, number of teeth	41.
,, ,, pitch-circle diameter	287 mm.
,, ,, width of teeth	75.0 mm.
,, ,, depth of teeth	15.1 mm.
,, ,, thickness of web (mean)	7.0 mm.
,, ,, extension, external diameter	75.0 mm.
,, ,, ,, internal diameter	50.0 mm.
,, ,, ,, number of splines	6.
,, ,, ,, depth of splines	4.0 mm.
Oil retaining rings, width	16.0 mm.
,, ,, ,, pitch of thread	1.25 mm.

BEARINGS.

BEARING No 1 (propeller end).

Type	Roller.
Rollers, number	18.
,, diameter	22.0 mm.
,, width	20.0 mm.
Journal, diameter	100.0 mm.
Bronze housing, external diameter	190.0 mm.
,, ,, internal diameter	180.0 mm.

BEARING No. 2 (centre).

Type	Roller and double thrust.
Rollers, number	20.
,, diameter	18.0 mm.
,, width	19.0 mm.
Journal, diameter	90.0 mm.
Double thrust race, balls, number	18 each.
,, ,, ,, ,, diameter	17.46 mm.
Bronze housing, external diameter	168.0 mm.
,, ,, internal diameter	160.0 mm.
,, ,, flange bolts, material	Aluminium alloy (see analysis).
,, ,, ,, ,, number	12.
,, ,, ,, ,, diameter	8.0 mm.
,, ,, ,, ,, pitch (threads)	1.25 mm.

BEARING No. 3 (front end).

Type	Roller.
Rollers, number	20
,, diameter	14.0 mm.
,, width	16.0 mm.
Journal, diameter	75.0 mm.
Bronze housing, external diameter	140.0 mm.
,, ,, internal diameter	130.0 mm.
Flange, diameter	185.0 mm.
,, thickness	12.0 mm.
,, bolts, diameter	18.0 mm.
,, ,, pitch diameter	150.0 mm.
Number of bolts	10
Shaft diameter, external	92.0 mm.
,, ,, internal	82.0 mm.

PROPELLER HUB.

Fixed and loose flanges, diameter	260.0 mm.
,, ,, ,, ,, thickness	8.0 mm.
Bolts, number	10
,, diameter	15.0 mm.
,, pitch circle diameter	220.0 mm.
Hub diameter, external	90.0 mm.
,, ,, internal	68.0 mm.
Splines, number	4
,, depth	5.0 mm.

CASING.

Gear Case Portion.

Thickness of casing (mean)	6.0 mm.
Gear case bolts, number	10
,, ,, ,, diameter	11.0 mm
,, ,, ,, pitch (threads)	1.5 mm.

NOSE PORTION.

Thickness of casing (mean)	6 mm.
Diameter of propeller end	280.0 mm.
,, ,, gear case end	350.0 mm.
Flange, diameter	394.0 mm.
,, thickness	10.0 mm.
,, bolts, material	Aluminium.
,, ,, number	12
,, ,, diameter	8.0 mm.
,, ,, pitch (threads)	1.25 mm.

OVERALL DIMENSIONS.

Length	1,025.0 mm.
Width	675.0 mm.
Depth	535.0 mm.

FLEXIBLE COUPLING.

(MALE PORTION.)

Outside diameter	304 mm.
Width	66 mm.
Material	Aluminium.

Recesses for leather blocks.

Number	8
Depth	11 mm
Width	51 mm.

(FEMALE PORTION ON FLYWHEEL.)

Inside diameter	308 mm.
Width (effective)	69 mm.
Material	Aluminium

Recesses for leather blocks.

Number	8
Depth	6 mm.
Width	51 mm.

SPLINE DRIVE FOR COUPLING.

(MALE PORTION.)

Number of splines	16
Outside diameter	100 mm.
Width	10 mm.
Length	20 mm.
Depth	4 mm.
Material	Steel.

OIL PUMP.

Type of pump	Gear.
Diameter of gears	28 mm.
Number of teeth	12 mm.
Width of teeth	18 mm.
Ratio of engine speed/oil pump drive	10.1.
Normal speed of pump	140 R.P.M.
Delivery of pump	See test report.
Diameter of delivery pipe	9 mm.

OIL RADIATOR.

Number of tubes	67
Diameter ,, ,, (inside)	24 mm.
Length ,, ,,	110 mm.
Thickness ,,	.5 mm.
Area of tube surface	5,556.9 sq. cm
Total area of cooling surface	7,101.36 sq. cm.
Thickness of plates	.75 mm.
Diameter of inlet pipe	25.0 mm.

F. G. C.

Lieut. R.A.F.

T.P.

(R.A.E.) June, 1919.

H. R. BROOKE POPHAM,

Brigadier General,

Director of Research.

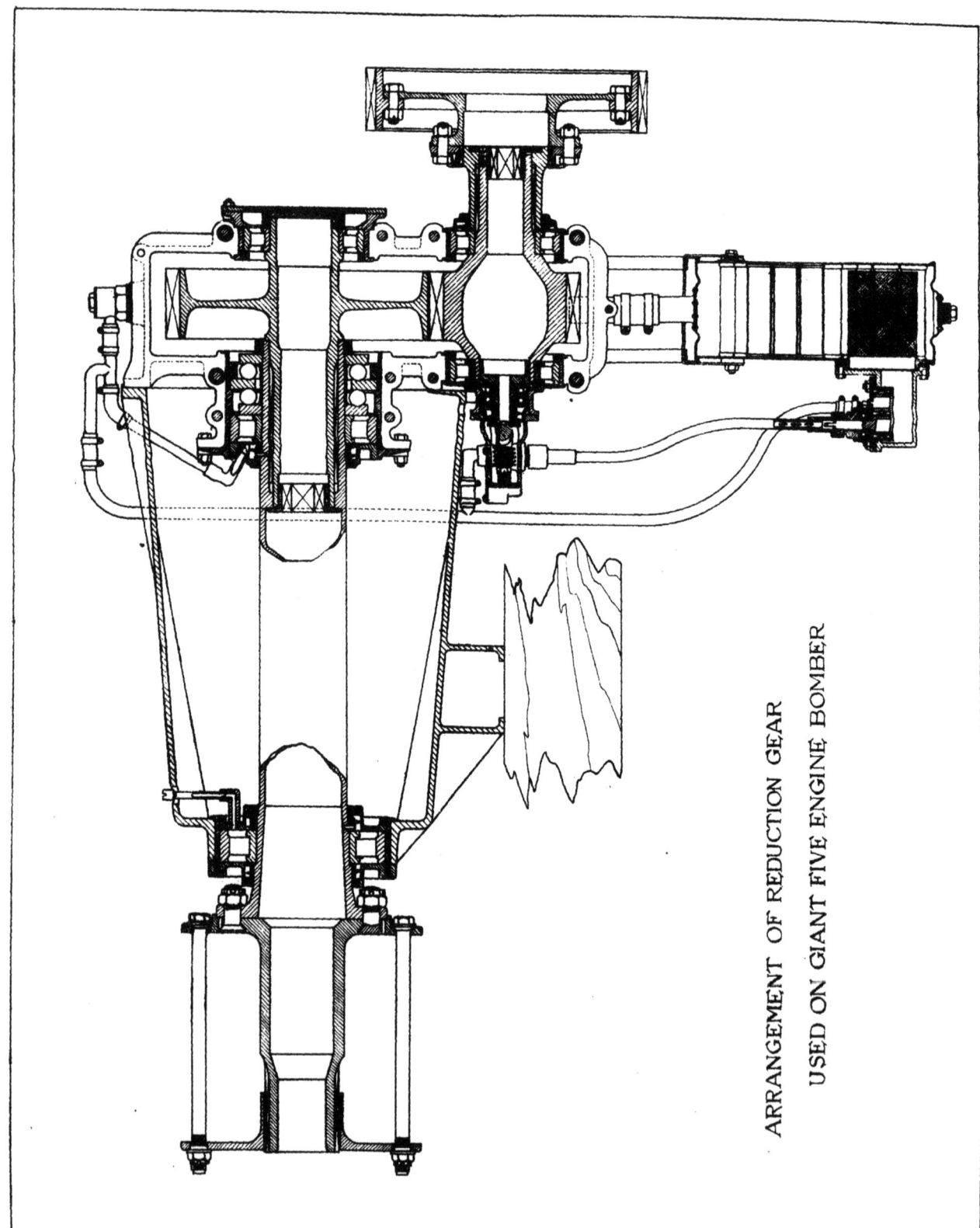

FIG. 12.

ARRANGEMENT OF REDUCTION GEAR
USED ON GIANT FIVE ENGINE BOMBER

(For dimensions see pages 10, 11 and 12.)